U.S. Department of Justice
Office of Justice Programs
Office of Juvenile Justice and Delinquency Prevention

Working for Youth Justice and Safety

OJJDP JUVENILE JUSTICE BULLETIN

December 2012

Melodee Hanes, Acting Administrator

Pathways to Desistance

How and why do many serious adolescent offenders stop offending while others continue to commit crimes? This series of bulletins presents findings from the Pathways to Desistance study, a multidisciplinary investigation that attempts to answer this question.

Investigators interviewed 1,354 young offenders from Philadelphia and Phoenix for 7 years after their convictions to learn what factors (e.g., individual maturation, life changes, and involvement with the criminal justice system) lead youth who have committed serious offenses to persist in or desist from offending.

As a result of these interviews and a review of official records, researchers have collected the most comprehensive dataset available about serious adolescent offenders and their lives in late adolescence and early adulthood.

These data provide an unprecedented look at how young people mature out of offending and what the justice system can do to promote positive changes in the lives of these youth.

Transfer of Juveniles to Adult Court: Effects of a Broad Policy in One Court

Edward P. Mulvey and Carol A. Schubert

Highlights

This bulletin presents findings from the Pathways to Desistance study about the effects of transfer from juvenile court to adult court on a sample of serious adolescent offenders in Maricopa County, AZ. The authors compare the extant literature with findings from the Pathways study and discuss the possible implications of these findings for future changes in transfer statutes. Following are some key points:

- Adolescents in the adult system may be at risk for disruptions in their personal development, identity formation, relationships, learning, growth in skills and competencies, and positive movement into adult status.

- Most of the youth in the study who were sent to adult facilities returned to the community within a few years, varying widely in their levels of adjustment. Youth were more likely to successfully adjust when they were not influenced by antisocial peers.

- Prior work indicates that transferred youth are more likely to commit criminal acts than adolescents kept in the juvenile justice system.

- Findings from the Pathways study indicate that transfer may have a differential effect (either reducing or increasing offending), depending on the juvenile's presenting offense and prior offense history.

DECEMBER 2012

Transfer of Juveniles to Adult Court: Effects of a Broad Policy in One Court

Edward P. Mulvey and Carol A. Schubert

Transferring an adolescent offender to adult court is a weighty decision. It has far-reaching implications for the adolescent involved and significant symbolic meaning for the justice system. For the adolescent, transfer to the adult system holds the possibility of harsher punishment (including physical, sexual, or psychological victimization by other inmates) and enduring developmental costs (Chung, Little, and Steinberg, 2005; Mulvey and Schubert, 2012). For the system, transferring an adolescent to adult court is an unambiguous statement that the criminal justice system will no longer shelter the adolescent, by virtue of his or her acts, from harsh justice. Transfer to adult court indicates that the demand for proportional punishment has trumped the goal of individualized rehabilitation found in the juvenile justice system (Zimring, 2005).

Since the court's inception, juvenile justice policymakers and professionals have wrestled with the decision about when to transfer an adolescent to adult court (Tanenhaus, 2004). Currently, individual states have combinations of statutorily defined mechanisms for determining when the movement of a juvenile case to adult court is required or appropriate, including procedures such as judicial transfer, certification, automatic waiver, or direct file (Griffin, 2003; Fagan and Zimring, 2000). In general, state statutes define a set of crimes for adolescent offenders of a certain age that warrant processing in the adult system (i.e., a statutory exclusion from the presumed jurisdiction of the juvenile court). Most states also have a mechanism (e.g., decertification, reverse waiver) for returning the case to the jurisdiction of the juvenile court when deemed appropriate. (See Sickmund, 1994; Griffin, 2006; and Redding, 2008, for an elaboration of these statutory provisions.)

Statutory standards have not always driven the process of transferring an adolescent to adult court. For most of the history of the juvenile court, the decision to transfer an adolescent offender to the adult court rested primarily on the discretion of the juvenile court judge. Since the inception of the juvenile court in 1899, transfer was possible for a range of "heinous" offenses when the juvenile court judge deemed that the resources available to the court were insufficient to rehabilitate an adolescent (Tanenhaus, 2000).

During the late 1980s and early 1990s, however, a sharp rise in violent crime produced intense interest in the causes of juvenile crime and the effectiveness of the juvenile justice system. Juvenile arrests for violent offenses jumped dramatically during this time period, increasing 64 percent nationally between 1980 and 1994 (Butts and Travis, 2002). In addition, some highly publicized cases of juveniles committing repeated, serious violent offenses contributed to public perception that the juvenile justice system was inadequate to intervene effectively with adolescents who were a legitimate threat to public safety (Butterfield, 1995). These forces even prompted radical, and ultimately unfounded, rhetoric about a coming wave of adolescent "superpredators" unlike any previous juvenile offenders in their heartlessness and lack of response to interventions (DiIulio, 1995).

In this context, the public began to distrust the ability of the juvenile justice system to ensure public safety, and state legislatures added statutory provisions to ensure that youth who committed certain serious offenses were not roaming the streets. Between 1992 and 1999, all but one state expanded legislation that made it easier for juveniles to be tried as adults (Hansen, 2001). These changes increased the set of crimes that qualified an adolescent for transfer, lifted age restrictions, and added statutory exclusion and prosecutorial discretion as methods for achieving transfer to adult court. The movement of adolescents to adult court was no longer the product of a juvenile court judge exercising his or her discretion; it was instead largely the product of who fell into the statutorily defined net of eligibility and was not waived back to juvenile court. Rather than relying on a judgment of individual appropriateness regarding transfer, the emphasis was instead on the act, not the actor, and on retribution, not rehabilitation (Griffin, 2006).

Effects of Changes in Transfer Policies on Practice

It is generally believed that these statutory reforms produced an increase in the rate of transfer, at least in a large number of locales (Fagan, 2008; Penney and Moretti, 2005). However, it is difficult to gauge the specific effects of these changes because of the lack of comprehensive and consistent data about transferred adolescent offenders. No systematic national count of the number of youth who are transferred or waived to criminal court exists, nor are there consistent data on the characteristics of these adolescents across locales. The National Center for Juvenile Justice tracks judicial transfers made at the discretion of juvenile court judges. These figures show a clear decline in adolescent transfers using this mechanism, presumably because other statutory mechanisms have increased their rate of transfer (Adams and Addie, 2010). However, no accurate tallies of the total number of transfers across all possible mechanisms exists.

The sources for estimating the number of adolescents in adult prisons or jails on any given day or during any given period of time are also inconsistent (Woolard et al., 2005). According to available data, the number and proportion of adolescents in adult prisons appear to have peaked in the mid-1990s (about 5,000 prisoners, or 2.3 percent of the total prison population, according to Hartney, 2006) and to have fallen since then to less than 3,000, or 1.2 percent, in 2004 (Hartney, 2006; see Austin, Johnson, and Gregoriou, 2000, for somewhat larger estimates for the mid-1990s). Estimates of the number of adolescents in adult jails on any given day are considerably greater, ranging from about 7,000 (Hartney, 2006) to 19,000 (Austin, Johnson, and Gregoriou, 2000)—about 1 in 10 youth incarcerated in the United States are admitted to an adult prison or jail (Eggleston, 2007).

In addition, little is actually known about outcomes for adolescent offenders who are transferred to the adult system. The Bureau of Justice Statistics (BJS) funded a recent study to compile available information about the number of adolescents who were transferred across a range of locales and the subsequent sanctions these individuals received. Study results are anticipated in 2012 and are expected to be "the best national estimates ever, and the most detailed exploration of who the kids are and what actually happens to them" (Kelly, 2010, p. 31).

Despite the lack of definitive numeric estimates, it is reasonable to assume that the changes in transfer statutes have led to an increase in the heterogeneity of the youth sent to adult court in many locales (Schubert et al., 2010). That is, expansions of the transfer statutes and an increased reliance on the presenting offense have made it easier for the adult court to process a broader range of adolescents; these adolescents likely differ widely in their prior legal involvement, developmental status (because there is now a wider age span for youth who are eligible for transfer), and specific risk factors related to offending. In general, researchers believe that the group of adolescents now transferred to adult court includes "a broad range of offenders who are neither particularly serious nor particularly chronic" (Bishop and Frazier, 2000, p. 265).

Reconsideration of the Current Transfer Policy

The wisdom of current transfer policies has been widely questioned, and some have begun to voice two major concerns about the potential impacts of these practices (Fagan and Zimring, 2000; Redding, 2008). The first concern is about fairness: Does placement in adult court expose adolescents to punishments and conditions that are unduly harsh? The second concern is about utility: Does the practice of juvenile transfer to adult court actually reduce crime as compared with placement in juvenile court?

Possible Detrimental Effects of Transfer

This section discusses some of the detrimental effects of transferring juveniles to adult court.

Longer Sentences

One potentially harmful outcome for transferred adolescent offenders is a longer or harsher sentence than they might have experienced if they had remained in the juvenile justice system. Both sides of the political spectrum seem to believe that this is the case. Those in favor of "get tough" policies promote long sentences for youth and see transfer to the adult system as a method to achieve this end. Meanwhile, those opposing adult sentences for juveniles imply that transfer to adult court produces long confinement in an adult facility.

Although clearly there are adolescents who receive extended stays in adult correctional facilities that could not be imposed on them if they stayed in the juvenile justice system, the overall impact of transfer on extending institutional confinement for all adolescents involved in

this process is not totally clear. For one thing, about 20 percent of transferred adolescent offenders receive probation in adult court (Bishop, 2000). For those who receive adult sentences, some evidence exists that juveniles who are transferred receive harsher or more punitive sentences compared with those who remain in the juvenile justice system (Kupchik, Fagan, and Liberman, 2003; Kurlychek and Johnson, 2004; Myers, 2003), possibly because the mere knowledge that a youth was transferred may convey a heightened level of risk to the judge, who may address it through a longer sentence (Kurlychek and Johnson, 2010). Males (2008), however, tracked 35,000 releasees from the California Department of Juvenile Justice and reported that juveniles were released from the adult system after a shorter time served than youth who were sentenced for the same offenses in the juvenile justice system.

Whatever the increased chance of extended incarceration might be with processing in the adult court, it is still clear that many adolescents who are processed in adult court are not necessarily confined for extended periods but, instead, come back to the community while they are still young adults. Redding (1999, citing a 1996 Texas study) reports that, although 87 percent of a sample of 946 juveniles received longer sentences in criminal court than they would have received in juvenile court, the average prison time actually served was only 3.5 years (an average of about 27 percent of the sentence imposed). In addition, BJS estimated that 78 percent of persons who were younger than age 18 when admitted to a state prison in 1997 would be released by age 21 (Strom, 2000). Whether or not they receive harsher sentences, the majority of adolescents transferred to the adult court are nonetheless coming back to the community during their early adulthood.

Victimization

Victimization in adult jail or prison presents another very real and troubling possibility for adolescents processed in

the adult system. The idea that other inmates or guards may subject adolescent offenders to physical, sexual, or psychological victimization because they are confined in adult facilities gives pause to even the most ardent supporters of retribution as a justification for transfer. As Mulvey and Schubert (2012) note, "Doing the time for doing the crime might be seen as fair, but doing much worse time because the crime was done while an adolescent seems to tip the balance beyond even-handed justice" (p. 846).

The available evidence points to the conclusion that adolescents are at increased risk of being physically or sexually victimized when they are housed in adult facilities. Even though adolescents represent only a small proportion of inmates in adult facilities, in 2005, 21 percent of all victims of substantiated incidents of inmate-on-inmate sexual violence in jails were juveniles younger than age 18 (Beck and Harrison, 2008). In addition, Beyer (1997) states that juveniles in adult facilities are five times more likely to be sexually assaulted and two times more likely to be beaten by staff than youth held in juvenile facilities (see also Feld, 1977, for a discussion of violence in juvenile settings). These estimates, however, are based on limited data. Interviews of inmates that BJS researchers conducted indicate that the annual prevalence of sexual assaults in juvenile facilities may range from 12 percent (Beck, Harrison, and Guerino, 2010) to 20 percent (*National Prison Rape Elimination Commission Report,* 2009). In contrast, other survey data by Fagan and Kupchik (as cited in Fagan, 2008, p. 101) indicate that in the juvenile facilities examined, the rates of reported physical violence were greater than the rates that adolescents in adult facilities reported. Although the exact amount of increased risk of assault may be in question, the studies in this area generally document that the risk of assault for a juvenile in an adult facility is substantially greater than the risk for an adult in the same facility.

The fact that an adolescent is at increased risk for assault in an adult facility is not surprising—placements in prisons and jails put relatively immature and inexperienced adolescents into a social environment that requires a tough

"Adolescents transferred to the adult system can experience harmful disruptions in their development during late adolescence and early adulthood."

exterior to survive. Such an arrangement seems to inevitably increase an adolescent's chances of being involved in a physical confrontation, either through efforts to establish a reputation or to resist assaults or sexual advances (Lane et al., 2002; McShane and Williams, 1989). The exact amount of increased risk of victimization is difficult to estimate, however, given the inadequacies of the data available and the tenuous validity of comparing datasets collected in different ways (Mulvey and Schubert, 2012).

Disruptions in Development

In addition to the immediate physical and psychological dangers resulting from incarceration, adolescents transferred to the adult system can also experience harmful disruptions in their development during late adolescence and early adulthood. Adolescent offenders can be assumed to be particularly diverse, and potentially delayed, in many aspects of social development (Monahan et al., 2009). Also, considerable evidence exists that prison and jail environments present challenges to one's sense of self and identity that even hardened criminals find disorienting, upsetting, and traumatic. Particularly vulnerable adolescents are thus taking the next steps of their developmental journey in an environment that does not promote physical or emotional health and that may harm their progress as well. Although an adolescent and an adult might receive what appears to be an equivalent sentence for a similar crime (e.g., 3 years for a felony assault), adolescents are paying for their crimes at a different point in their life journey; the impact of this experience may be more dramatic as a result.

Identity formation is one of the most salient processes of adolescent development that incarceration might affect. To fashion a sense of self (i.e., to figure out who one is in relation to family and others, as well as what one's future might hold), most adolescents follow a pattern of individuating from parents, orienting toward peers, and integrating components of attitudes and behavior into an autonomous self-identity (Collins and Steinberg, 2006). The last stage of this process involves choosing the identity that actually "fits" from the many that might have been "tried on"—as

well as reconciling and consolidating what the person might want to be (the idealized self) with what the person might worry about being or becoming (the feared self) (Oyserman and Fryberg, 2006). Navigating this developmental period successfully requires supportive adults, healthy relationships with peers, and opportunities to make autonomous decisions (Scott and Steinberg, 2008).

Adolescents in adult facilities try to accomplish this developmental task in environments that present very real dangers to their safety; this is hardly an environment in which experimentation with a wide range of self-presentations or alternative viewpoints can be pursued with impunity. Instead, the pervasive influence of prisonization—adaptation to prison through identification with the role of being a criminal among criminals (Clemmer, 1958; Gillespie, 2003)—can be expected to undermine healthy identity development. In addition, the likelihood of receiving positive support for identity development from either peers or adults in these settings seems low. Peer relationships often offer little more than "schooling" that is useful for later criminality (Maruna and Toch, 2005), and adult relationships are likely to be negative. In the end, prisons and jails are primarily designed to break down identities, not foster new, resilient ones that are adaptive to the world outside the facility walls. Adolescents in these settings are forming a sense of who they are in an environment that tells them they should not trust anyone and they should not try to be different.

Adolescents in the adult system also often lose critical opportunities for learning in late adolescence. By definition, adolescence marks the transition period between childhood and adulthood during which an individual progresses toward adult levels of responsibility and adult roles. Adolescents gradually take greater control over an expanding range of life decisions; they also make mistakes, pick up pointers, and learn lessons along the way. According to Zimring (2005), during this period adolescents are operating with a "learner's permit" for developing maturity; they are generally under the watchful eye of caring individuals and are afforded more tolerance from society for making bad choices.

Spending time in prison or jail, however, curtails the amount of an adolescent's "practice time" to freely develop skills and competencies in several areas. Learning about job-related expectations, gaining résumé-building skills, discovering qualities in a potential life partner, learning how to spend unstructured time, and learning to manage a household are not easily acquired behavioral repertoires—they require some trial and error. The regimented and highly structured schedules and restrictions in jail and prison environments, however, at best reduce opportunities to develop lasting romantic relationships, identify career interests, or develop work skills. Even the most progressive of these environments (e.g., specialized young adult offender programs) cannot provide experiences as broad as those provided to unconfined youth.

Do Transfer Policies Reduce Crime?

Over the past two decades, researchers and policymakers have become increasingly interested in whether expanded statutory guidelines for juvenile transfers to adult court have actually reduced overall criminal offending by transferred adolescents or juvenile crime more generally. There are a number of ways in which such statutory guidelines could affect crime levels. First, locking up serious offenders could reduce crime because highly criminally active adolescents are removed from the streets during the years they would be committing these crimes (incapacitation). Second, tougher and more inclusive transfer policies could deter future crime; i.e., adolescent offenders transferred to adult court might refrain from future offending because they have learned that the criminal justice system will impose a harsh penalty if they offend seriously again (specific deterrence). In addition, other adolescents, although not transferred themselves, might reduce their offending because they are aware that harsher penalties are in place, thus making the cost of continued offending unacceptably high (general deterrence).

There is no solid empirical information about the potential effects of incapacitation on the offending of adolescents transferred to adult court. Such analyses would require estimates of the amount of crime that these individuals might have committed compared with the incapacitation effect that might have been obtained if these same individuals had remained in the juvenile justice system. Although some analyses indicate that increased incarceration rates have produced some incapacitation effect (Spelman, 2000), the amount of crime reduction attributable to expanded transfer policies is unclear. There is some reason to be skeptical that the effect would be large because the level of incapacitation achieved from incarceration depends on whether the most criminally active individuals are being confined. This is a questionable assumption, given that transfer statutes are based primarily on the current offense rather than the overall risk and chronicity of offending (Redding, 2008).

It is also unclear whether a general deterrence effect exists that is attributable to more stringent transfer statutes. Jensen and Metsger (1994), using a time-series approach, found a 13-percent increase in arrest rates for violent juvenile crime in Idaho after the implementation of an automatic transfer statute. Singer and colleagues (Singer and McDowell, 1988; Singer, 1996) found that a New York statute that automatically sends violent juvenile offenders to adult court had no deterrent effect on overall juvenile crime, even though the law was widely applied and publicized in the media. In contrast, Levitt (1998) conducted an econometrically oriented, multistate study that found support for a deterrence effect. In these analyses, the investigators found an estimated 25-percent decrease in violent juvenile crime and a 10- to 15-percent decrease in property crime that juveniles committed in states that had lowered the age of jurisdiction for transfer to adult court. The largest effects were in states with the greatest disparity in the severity of punishment between the adult and juvenile courts. Levitt's study is notable for its unique methodological approach; it examined the associations between the statutory age of jurisdiction and observed crime rates rather than conducting a more typical analysis of crimes in comparable samples. Overall, the amount of research supporting or refuting general deterrence effects is extremely sparse and inconclusive (McGowan et al., 2007).

More work has been done regarding the specific deterrence effects of juvenile transfers to adult court; numerous

"Youth who associate with more antisocial peers resume antisocial activity more quickly and are rearrested more quickly than those who have more positive social relationships."

studies compare the arrest histories of samples of juvenile offenders processed in the juvenile justice system with those processed in the adult court system. For example, Fagan and colleagues (Fagan, 1996; Kupchik, Fagan, and Liberman, 2003) examined a natural experiment on the deterrent effects of juvenile versus adult court sanctions by comparing recidivism among 15- and 16-year-olds from two matched communities (one in New York and one in New Jersey) who were charged with robbery and burglary. The transfer laws for these crimes differed in the two states (New York has a lower age of criminal responsibility for adult court), permitting a comparison of outcomes for youth who live in otherwise comparable neighboring counties. The researchers found that for robbery offenders, transfer was associated with a greater likelihood of, and quicker time to, rearrest. Although significant, these effects could only be generalized to robbery offenses, as the authors found no such significant differences for burglary offenders. In another well-known study, Bishop and colleagues (1996) and Winner and colleagues (1997) estimated the effects of transfers on future recidivism in a sample of Florida juvenile transfer cases, as compared with nontransfer cases, after matching on seven factors (number and seriousness of charges, number and seriousness of prior convictions, age, race, and gender). The researchers found that transferred youth had an increased likelihood of recidivism and reoffended more quickly than their non-transferred counterparts. Finally, Myers (2003) analyzed outcomes for 494 youth from Pennsylvania, 79 of whom were transferred to adult court and 415 who were retained in juvenile court. Using statistical controls for selection bias, Myers also concluded that transferred youth had greater rates of recidivism.

Studies like these have contributed to the conclusion that juvenile transfer policies uniformly produce negative outcomes. Some scholars have indicated that transferred adolescents are more likely to recidivate, recidivate at a greater rate, and be rearrested for more serious offenses, on average, than those retained in the juvenile justice system (Bishop and Frazier, 2000). In addition, several reports have asserted that transfer laws are at the least ineffective (i.e., they do not prevent future crime among those transferred; see Redding, 2008) and may in fact be harmful (i.e., counterproductive for the purpose of reducing crime and enhancing public safety; see McGowan et al., 2007; Young and Gainsborough, 2000).

The Next Generation of Transfer Research

The studies on which these conclusions are based are impressive; however, like all research, they have some inevitable limitations. First, it is debatable whether this research has fully addressed the issue of sample selection when assessing the impact of being transferred to adult court or retained in juvenile court. A comparison of offenders who are transferred to adult court and those who are not transferred involves two groups that are inherently different in important ways that predate incarceration and that may affect any comparison of the groups' patterns of reoffending. Consequently, observed differences (e.g., greater arrest rates) in the transferred population cannot be accurately attributed to the transfer experience itself as long as these differences in outcomes might also be partially or fully attributable to fundamental differences between the transferred and retained youth. Prior work (e.g., Bishop et al., 1996; Winner et al., 1997) has controlled statistically for several factors (such as age, offense, and number of prior petitions) that might influence the likelihood that an individual's case will be transferred to criminal court and are associated with greater levels of future arrest. These efforts undoubtedly provide some level of correction for existing group differences. Because there is no random assignment to the "treatment condition" of juvenile transfer to adult court, however, there is always the question of whether these methods have provided enough control to make the two groups directly comparable on outcomes (Loughran and Mulvey, 2010).

ABOUT THE PATHWAYS TO DESISTANCE STUDY

The Pathways to Desistance study is a multidisciplinary, multisite longitudinal investigation of how serious juvenile offenders make the transition from adolescence to adulthood. It follows 1,354 young offenders from Philadelphia County, PA, and Maricopa County, AZ (metropolitan Phoenix), for 7 years after their conviction. This study has collected the most comprehensive dataset currently available about serious adolescent offenders and their lives in late adolescence and early adulthood. It looks at the factors that lead youth who have committed serious offenses to persist in or desist from offending. Among the aims of the study are to:

- Identify initial patterns of how serious adolescent offenders stop antisocial activity.

- Describe the role of social context and developmental changes in promoting these positive changes.

- Compare the effects of sanctions and interventions in promoting these changes.

Characteristics of Study Participants

Enrollment took place between November 2000 and March 2003, and the research team concluded data collection in 2010. In general, participating youth were at least 14 years old and younger than 18 years old at the time of their study index petition; 8 youth were 13 years old and 16 youth were older than age 18 but younger than 19 at the time of their index petition. The youth in the sample were adjudicated delinquent or found guilty of a serious (overwhelmingly felony-level) violent crime, property offense, or drug offense at their current court appearance. Although felony drug offenses are among the eligible charges, the study limited the proportion of male drug offenders to no more than 15 percent; this limit ensures a heterogeneous sample of serious offenders. Because investigators wanted to include a large enough sample of female offenders—a group neglected in previous research—this limit did not apply to female drug offenders. In addition, youth whose cases were considered for trial in the adult criminal justice system were enrolled, regardless of the offense committed.

At the time of their baseline interview, participants were an average of 16.5 years old. The sample was 84 percent male and 80 percent minority (41 percent black, 34 percent Hispanic, and 5 percent American Indian/other). For approximately one-quarter (25.5 percent) of study participants, the study index petition was their first petition to court. Of the remaining participants (those with a petition before the study index petition), 69 percent had 2 or more prior petitions; the average was 3 in Maricopa County and 2.8 in Philadelphia County (exclusive of the study index offense). At both sites, more than 40 percent of the adolescents enrolled were adjudicated of felony crimes against persons (i.e., murder, robbery, aggravated assault, sex offenses, and kidnapping). At the time of

the baseline interview for the study, 50 percent of these adolescents were in an institutional setting (usually a residential treatment center); during the 7 years after study enrollment, 87 percent of the sample spent some time in an institutional setting.

Interview Methodology

Immediately after enrollment, researchers conducted a structured 4-hour baseline interview (in two sessions) with each adolescent. This interview included a thorough assessment of the adolescent's self-reported social background, developmental history, psychological functioning, psychosocial maturity, attitudes about illegal behavior, intelligence, school achievement and engagement, work experience, mental health, current and previous substance use and abuse, family and peer relationships, use of social services, and antisocial behavior.

After the baseline interview, researchers interviewed study participants every 6 months for the first 3 years, and annually thereafter. At each followup interview, researchers gathered information on the adolescent's self-reported behavior and experiences during the previous 6-month or 1-year reporting period, including any illegal activity, drug or alcohol use, and involvement with treatment or other services. Youth's self-reports about illegal activities included information about the range, the number, and other circumstances of those activities (e.g., whether or not others took part). In addition, the follow-up interviews collected a wide range of information about changes in life situations (e.g., living arrangements, employment), developmental factors (e.g., likelihood of thinking about and planning for the future, relationships with parents), and functional capacities (e.g., mental health symptoms).

Researchers also asked participants to report monthly about certain variables (e.g., school attendance, work performance, and involvement in interventions and sanctions) to maximize the amount of information obtained and to detect activity cycles shorter than the reporting period.

In addition to the interviews of study participants, for the first 3 years of the study, researchers annually interviewed a family member or friend about the study participant to validate the participant's responses. Each year, researchers also reviewed official records (local juvenile and adult court records and FBI nationwide arrest records) for each adolescent.

Investigators have now completed the last (84-month) set of followup interviews, and the research team is conducting analyses of interview data. The study maintained the adolescents' participation throughout the project: At each followup interview point, researchers found and interviewed approximately 90 percent of the enrolled sample. Researchers have completed more than 21,000 interviews in all.

Second, this work focuses on the effects of transfer only in terms of the persistence of criminal involvement; the impact of transfer may also involve other social and developmental domains. For example, involvement with the adult court can affect facets of successful adjustment (e.g., employment and social relationships), either promoting or curtailing continued offending (Chung, Little, and Steinberg, 2005). Although the question of whether transfer increases or decreases the rate of future arrests is certainly a salient policy issue, it does not address the other effects on an adolescent's life and life chances.

Third, these studies have not rigorously and consistently considered the possibility of variation in subgroups. The transferred group might contain identifiable subgroups with different outcomes related to case characteristics. Certain identifiable groups of transferred adolescent offenders (e.g., those charged with particular types of crimes) might be more likely to have positive or negative outcomes. Some types of youth may be easily deterred (e.g., those with limited legal histories or who have positive peer support), whereas others may not consider the possibility of prison time a sufficient threat to desist from crime. Alternatively, certain malleable characteristics (e.g., association with antisocial peers, substance use) may be related to positive or negative outcomes among transferred adolescents, providing guidance about the factors that should be assessed for adolescents who are eligible for transfer and those who should be targeted for intervention. Unfortunately, studies about transfer to adult court have paid only cursory attention to this issue, usually comparing two broad groups: youth retained in the juvenile justice system versus those transferred to adult court. When variability was considered in these analyses, comparisons were usually made within groups formed on the basis of charged offenses (Fagan, 1996; Gottfredson and Gottfredson, 1986; Petersilia et al., 1985).

The final point is particularly relevant when fashioning future research studies. Expanded statutes that create a wider net to catch juvenile offenders for transfer to adult court will likely lead to an "inappropriate aggregation" (Zimring, 1998)—that is, different types of offenders, with different responses to transfer consequences, are inadvertently combined for analytic purposes. If marked variability exists in the effects of transfer on subgroups of those adolescents who are eligible to be transferred, then looking for a single effect across all transferred individuals is an inadequate way to evaluate the merits of transfer policy. A more realistic, and potentially valuable, method would be to see how juvenile transfer to adult court might have differential effects, depending on the characteristics of both the offender and the offense. For example, inexperienced offenders might respond very differently to criminal sanctions when compared with more seasoned offenders (Loughran et al., 2012; Pogarsky and Piquero,

2003). If, as asserted earlier, transfer to adult court is an enduring component of the criminal justice process, the core question is not whether transfer policy is "good" or "bad"; instead, the question is how to refine this practice to do more good and less harm. Thus, a "new generation" of research on this topic should provide information about differential outcomes for transferred youth and point to ways in which transfer statutes can more effectively target the appropriate groups of adolescents.

Analyses of Juvenile Transfer Using Data From the Pathways to Desistance Study

Pathways to Desistance[1] investigators and collaborators from the juvenile justice system in Maricopa County, AZ, examined the outcomes of transfer to adult court for youth enrolled in the Pathways study from that locale (see "About the Pathways to Desistance Study"). The goals of the analyses were (1) to describe the variability in outcomes for transferred youth and (2) to assess the effect of transfer to adult court, both overall and for subgroups of adolescents with different histories and who were convicted of different types of offenses. The approach used for the data analyses was developed in collaboration with juvenile court professionals, judges, and policymakers from Maricopa County; this addressed issues being discussed in Arizona at the time regarding possible changes in its transfer statute.

Data from the Pathways study were well suited to these tasks. First, the study captures a comprehensive array of information about serious adolescent offenders who are making the transition to adulthood—indicators of individual functioning, psychosocial development, family context, personal relationships, and community context—all of which have not been examined previously for this group. Second, it offers an opportunity to investigate juvenile transfer in one locale (Maricopa County, AZ) with a high rate of transfer to adult court, an example of what occurs when highly inclusive statutory guidelines are put into place.

The Sample

The analyses reported here used only cases enrolled in the Pathways study from Maricopa County, AZ. There are 654 adolescents in this Arizona sample; 193 (29 percent) of them were transferred to adult court. In the Philadelphia sample, there was a much lower rate of transfer to adult court; only 51 (7 percent) of the 700 enrollees were transferred to adult court for the offense that made them eligible for the study. The statutes in Arizona throw a wide net for transfer to adult court, and thus provide a reasonable test of the effects of a broad transfer statute on adolescent outcomes.

"There is no solid empirical information about the potential effects of incapacitation on the offending of adolescents transferred to adult court."

Under Arizona law, there are multiple paths (judicial, statutory, and prosecutorial) by which a youth can be transferred, there is a broad range of offenses that can produce automatic transfer, and the age of exclusion from juvenile court is in some situations quite young (e.g., 8 years old). Also, there is no provision for a hearing to return to juvenile court if an adolescent is charged with an offense eligible for transfer, and once a juvenile from Arizona has been prosecuted as an adult in criminal court, all subsequent cases involving that youth (regardless of the crime) come under adult criminal court jurisdiction. Six other states (California, Florida, Georgia, Louisiana, Oklahoma, and Vermont) offer the same range of transfer mechanisms, and nearly every other state has some combination of the options available in these states (Griffin, 2006).

Youth from the Pathways study who were transferred to adult court in Arizona were, on average, 17 years old, predominantly minority (59 percent Hispanic, 12 percent African American, 21 percent white, and 8 percent other), and overwhelmingly male (94 percent). The sample included 10 girls. This group had an average of three petitions to juvenile court prior to their baseline interview. Their first petition, on average, was at age 15, and 29 percent of the transferred youth had no court petitions prior to the offense qualifying them for inclusion in the study.

There were notable differences between the group of 193 adolescents transferred to adult court and the 461 participants retained in the Arizona juvenile court system. Those in the transferred group were significantly older at the time of enrollment, older at their first petition to court, had more prior petitions before the study baseline interview, were more likely to be members of a minority group, had parents with a lower level of education, and were involved with more antisocial peers.

The individuals studied here were followed from the time of study enrollment through their 4-year followup interview (average followup period = 1,544 days). During that 4-year period, a maximum of seven followup interviews could have been completed. Eighty-one percent (*n* = 156) of the 193 adolescents transferred to adult court completed all 7 followup interviews, and another 10 percent (*n* = 20) missed only 1 interview. Twenty-eight of these adolescents spent the entire 4-year followup period in a correctional facility as a result of the offense that qualified them for the study (these adolescents are excluded from later analyses of the community adjustment of the transferred youth).

What Happens to Transferred Adolescents?

A series of analyses (Schubert et al., 2010) describes the variability in the sample of 193 adolescents in Arizona who were transferred to adult court in terms of community outcomes. The measures of community outcomes were (1) arrest following release from the initial disposition stay, (2) subsequent overnight stay in a facility after the initial disposition stay, (3) reported participation in antisocial activities, and (4) participation in gainful activity, defined as either working or attending school. Researchers integrated information from the interviews with the adolescents and official records to calculate these outcome measures. Schubert and colleagues (2010) provide more information about the measures used for each outcome.

In addition to describing the prevalence of outcomes for these adolescents, the researchers also examined the case characteristics associated with different outcomes; i.e., they looked at whether particular case characteristics were associated with a greater likelihood of arrest, placement in an institution, self-reported antisocial activities, or participation in gainful activity. For these analyses, researchers assigned each case a set of risk-need factor scores that depicted the youth's status regarding a range of background characteristics known to be predictive of continued future offending (see Mulvey, Schubert, and Chung, 2007, for more details regarding the instruments used and the calculation of these scores). The risk-need scores calculated were (1) association with antisocial peers, (2) antisocial attitudes, (3) parental antisocial history, (4) school difficulties, (5) substance use problems, and (6) mood/anxiety problems. A series of regressions tested whether legal, demographic, psychological, and risk-need case characteristics predicted the time to occurrence of each of the outcomes.

Findings include the following:

- Youth who are transferred to the adult system do not always experience "hard time." Although 73 percent of this sample were incarcerated (either in prison or jail), 19 percent were placed on probation and 8 percent had their cases dismissed.

- Youth experience many challenges in the community while on probation or following release from an adult facility. Although the vast majority are involved in gainful activity quickly (within 2.5 months) and consistently (for nearly three-quarters of the months they spend in the community), the majority (77 percent) also resumed some level of antisocial activity and two-thirds were subsequently arrested or placed in an institutional setting. Only 18 of these youth (out of 193) managed to break out of this antisocial pattern completely.

- In this sample, prior history was strongly related to outcomes. Youth who were transferred to adult court at their first court petition were older and more mature; they also had a lower rate of rearrest and were more likely to return to gainful activity than those who had prior court petitions. The level of prior offending, even among transferred adolescents who committed more serious crimes, was related to subsequent adjustment in the community. Those with fewer prior petitions generally had significantly better outcomes than those who had more prior petitions to court.

- Legal factors (e.g., number of prior petitions, age at first prior offense, and whether the offense was a crime against a person) and the six risk-need factors predicted certain outcomes. However, psychological (e.g., IQ, measures of psychosocial maturity) and demographic (e.g., age, ethnicity, level of parental education) factors were not related to outcomes.

- Youth who associated with more antisocial peers resumed antisocial activity more quickly and were rearrested more quickly than those who had more positive social relationships. This supports the general contention that juveniles, even serious offenders who are transferred to adult court, are highly susceptible to negative peer influences and outside pressures.

How Does Transfer to Adult Court Affect Future Offending?

A second series of analyses (Loughran et al., 2010) builds on the initial descriptive work and tests whether similar youth (some transferred and some retained in the juvenile justice system) were more or less successful in the community. The research team used propensity score matching (Rosenbaum and Rubin, 1983) in these analyses to construct two groups of youth—one group that was transferred to adult court and another group that was retained in juvenile court—that had similar background characteristics. The outcomes for these two groups were then compared to see if being transferred to adult court had a positive or negative effect.

In this situation, the propensity score matching procedure first uses a wide variety of variables to construct a model that differentiates the cases transferred to adult court from those retained in the juvenile justice system. It then assigns each case a propensity score that reflects how much that individual case "looks like" a case that would be transferred to adult court. Each case that was actually transferred is then matched with a case that was not transferred but has the same propensity score. The groups constructed this way (i.e., the transferred group and the matched group) are then compared to make sure that they are equivalent on a variety of case characteristics. If they are similar on a large number of background characteristics, these factors can be eliminated as potential causes of any observed group differences on outcomes. In this set of analyses, the transferred group and the matched group (derived from propensity score matching) were equivalent on the case characteristics shown in the sidebar, "Characteristics With No Difference Between Matched Groups of Offenders" on page 12.

The adolescents transferred to adult court and the matched comparison group were compared on the outcomes of rearrest and self-reported involvement in antisocial activities. These analyses produced three principal findings:

- A review of the entire sample of transferred juveniles and their matched comparison cases in the juvenile justice system showed no effect of transfer on the rate of

rearrest. Unlike previous studies, the researchers found that when background characteristics (e.g., psychosocial maturity, risk-need indicators, emotional reactivity) were stringently controlled for, transfer to adult court did not raise the arrest rate appreciably.

- Despite this overall null effect, there was evidence of differential effects of transfer. Transferred adolescents

CHARACTERISTICS WITH NO DIFFERENCE BETWEEN MATCHED GROUPS OF OFFENDERS

When the researchers matched offenders whose cases were transferred to adult court with similar offenders whose cases were retained in juvenile court, they found no difference in the following sets of characteristics:

- **Demographic:** Age, gender, race/ethnicity (white/black/Hispanic/other), parents' education.

- **Household composition:** One/both biological parents present.

- **Intelligence:** IQ.

- **Employment:** Employed.

- **Official record information:** Number of prior petitions, age at first prior petition.

- **Gang involvement.**

- **Number of early onset behavior problems.**

- **Services:** Any overnight stays in a facility, any involvement in community service.

- **Risk-need factors:** Antisocial history/attitudes, mood/anxiety problems, parental antisocial history, association with antisocial peers, school difficulties, substance use problems.

- **Trait anxiety:** Total anxiety score (Revised Child Manifest Anxiety Scale).

- **Substance use and mental health disorders:** Alcohol/drug abuse or dependency, presence of a selected mental health diagnosis.

- **Psychopathy:** Psychopathy checklist factors 1 and 2.

- **Acculturation:** Overall/affirmation and belonging/identity achievement (multigroup measure of ethnic identity).

- **Exposure to violence as a victim/witness.**

- **Psychological development:** Weinberger Adjustment Inventory—consideration of others, impulse control, suppression of anger, temperament; Psychosocial Maturity Index; resistance to peer influence.

- **Emotional reactivity:** Self-regulation (Children's Emotion Regulation scale).

- **Social and personal costs and rewards of punishment:** Certainty of punishment (self/others), cost of punishment (variety/freedom issues/material issues), social costs of punishment, personal rewards to crime.

- **Perceptions of procedural justice.**

- **Social support:** Domains of social support (number).

- **Academic motivation:** Motivation to succeed.

- **Moral disengagement.**

- **Involvement in community activities:** Past 6 months (percent).

- **Number of unsupervised routine activities.**

- **Personal capital and social ties:** Social capital (closure and integration/perceived opportunity for work/social integration).

Notes:

Revised Child Manifest Anxiety Scale: A 37-item self-report instrument used to assess the level and nature of anxiety (Reynolds and Richmond, 1985).

Psychopathy checklist (PCL) factors 1 and 2: The PCL is a 20-item scale that is frequently divided into 2 factors. Factor 1 is composed of items assessing interpersonal style and factor 2 assesses antisocial behavior (Forth, Kosson, and Hare, 2003; Jones et al., 2006; Cooke and Michie, 2001).

Weinberger Adjustment Inventory: A scale used to assess an individual's social-emotional adjustment (i.e., impulse control, suppression of aggression, consideration of others, and temperance) (Weinberger and Schwartz, 1990).

Psychosocial Maturity Index: A scale used to assess personal responsibility (i.e., self-reliance, identity, and work orientation) (Greenberger et al., 1974).

Children's Emotion Regulation scale: A scale used to obtain a self-report assessment of the adolescent's ability to regulate emotions (Walden, Harris, and Catron, 2003).

charged with crimes against persons (e.g., felony assault, robbery) showed lower rates of rearrest, and transferred adolescents charged with property crimes (e.g., burglary) showed greater rates of rearrest (see figure below). These effects were present even after controlling for other factors that were statistically significantly different between the juveniles transferred to adult court and those retained in the juvenile justice system. The figure illustrates the differences in the rearrest rates for each group.

- Individuals with either no prior petitions or one prior petition fared better in terms of being rearrested, regardless of court jurisdiction (i.e., adult or juvenile court).

Discussion of Findings

The findings reported in this bulletin are compelling because they extend the story regarding what is known about juveniles transferred to adult court while addressing some limitations in previous investigations. The sample is composed entirely of serious juvenile offenders; the outcomes observed and the comparison cases considered are highly appropriate for examining the impact of transfer. These are the adolescents who are most likely to be transferred to adult court. Because the datasets are comprehensive, the researchers were able to rule out a wide range of possibly confounding factors; this is an improvement over much of the existing research, which contains more limited data (Kurlychek and Johnson, 2010). Perhaps most important, the Pathways data provide a unique opportunity to more fully explore the issue of heterogeneity among transferred individuals, the importance of which other researchers have emphasized (Bishop, 2000; Zimring, 1998). A considerable amount of variability exists within the Pathways sample of transferred youth in Arizona in both legal and certain risk-need factors as well as adjustment following involvement in the adult court system.

It is important to remember, however, that these analyses reflect regularities in one locale only. The use of data from Maricopa County illustrates the processes that would probably be seen in other metropolitan areas with highly inclusive transfer policies. At the same time, different results may be obtained in different locales with different types of offenders or different practices. More research on these differences is clearly needed.

Despite this limitation, findings across both sets of analyses still highlight the following points relevant to locales with high rates of transfer to adult court. First, transferred youth do come back to the community and most of them continue to be involved in criminal behavior. Following release from an adult facility or while on probation, these youth managed to return to school or work. However, nearly half of the released youth reported engaging in persistent antisocial activity, and about two-thirds were rearrested or returned to an institutional setting. At the same time, these results indicate that some characteristics related to these negative outcomes (e.g., antisocial attitudes, association with antisocial peers) could be targets for intervention when these young people return to the community.

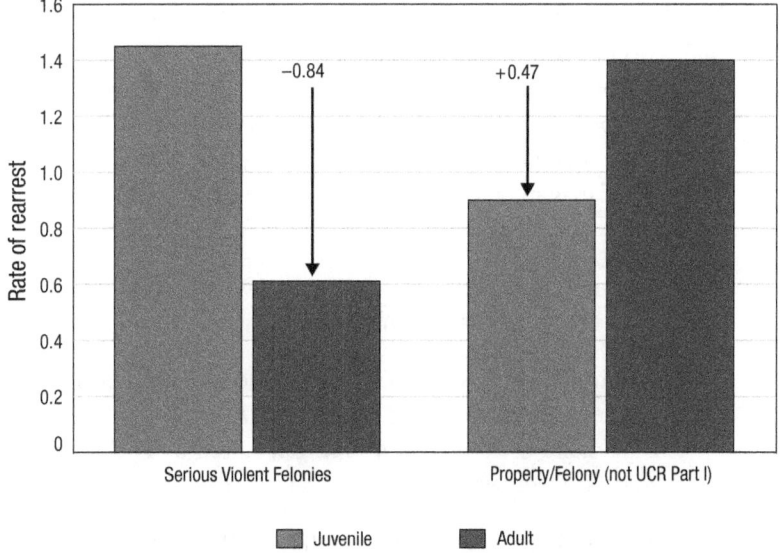

Rearrest Rates by Arresting Offense Group (Matched Samples)

Note: Youth in the Pathways study who were sent to the adult system for a serious violent felony offense (excluding sex offenses) had a subsequent arrest rate that was 0.84 less than those who remained in the juvenile justice system. Youth in the Pathways study who were sent to the adult system for a property offense or another felony (other than Uniform Crime Reports (UCR) Part I and excluding drug offenses) had a subsequent arrest rate that was 0.47 greater than those who remained in the juvenile justice system.

Second, this work suggests ways to refine the groups who are eligible for transfer so that transfer policy can be more limited and effective. These analyses provide clear evidence that certain case characteristics, most notably type of offense and prior history, are differentially related to outcomes among transferred adolescents. Transfer seems to have its intended effect with serious violent offenders, but it has a detrimental effect with serious property offenders. Similarly, serious adolescent offenders with no prior petitions are likely to increase their rearrest rate if transferred, compared with adolescents retained in the juvenile justice system. Taken together, these issues provide a springboard for discussions about how to improve current practices, and whether adolescents charged with certain types of offenses might be more successful and law-abiding if they remain in the juvenile justice system. These are the next challenging topics for discussion when considering reasonable reforms to the practice of transferring juveniles to adult court.

Endnotes

1. OJJDP is sponsoring the Pathways to Desistance study (Project Number 2007–MU–FX–0002) in partnership with the National Institute of Justice (Project Number 2008–IJ–CX–0023), the John D. and Catherine T. MacArthur Foundation, the William T. Grant Foundation, the Robert Wood Johnson Foundation, the William Penn Foundation, the National Institute on Drug Abuse (Grant Number R01DA019697), the Centers for Disease Control and Prevention, the Pennsylvania Commission on Crime and Delinquency, and the Arizona State Governor's Justice Commission. Investigators for this study are Edward P. Mulvey, Ph.D. (University of Pittsburgh), Robert Brame, Ph.D. (University of North Carolina–Charlotte), Elizabeth Cauffman, Ph.D. (University of California–Irvine), Laurie Chassin, Ph.D. (Arizona State University), Sonia Cota-Robles, Ph.D. (Temple University), Jeffrey Fagan, Ph.D. (Columbia University), George Knight, Ph.D. (Arizona State University), Sandra Losoya, Ph.D. (Arizona State University), Alex Piquero, Ph.D. (Florida State University), Carol A. Schubert, M.P.H. (University of Pittsburgh), and Laurence Steinberg, Ph.D. (Temple University). More details about the study can be found in a previous OJJDP fact sheet (Mulvey, 2011) and at the study Web site (www.pathwaysstudy.pitt.edu), which includes a list of publications from the study.

References

Adams, B., and Addie, S. 2010. *Delinquency Cases Waived to Criminal Court, 2007.* Washington, DC: U.S. Department of Justice, Office of Justice Programs, Office of Juvenile Justice and Delinquency Prevention.

Austin, J., Johnson, K., and Gregoriou, M. 2000. *Juveniles in Adult Prisons and Jails: A National Assessment.* Washington, DC: U.S. Department of Justice, Office of Justice Programs, Bureau of Justice Assistance.

Beck, A., and Harrison, P.M. 2008. *Sexual Victimization in State and Federal Prisons Reported by Inmates, 2007.* Washington, DC: U.S. Department of Justice, Office of Justice Programs, Bureau of Justice Statistics.

Beck, A., Harrison, P.M., and Guerino, P. 2010. *Sexual Victimization in Juvenile Facilities Reported by Youth, 2008–09.* Washington, DC: U.S. Department of Justice, Office of Justice Programs, Bureau of Justice Statistics.

Beyer, M. 1997. Experts for juveniles at risk of adult sentences. In *More Than Meets the Eye: Rethinking Assessment, Competency and Sentencing for a Harsher Era of Juvenile Justice,* edited by P. Puritz, A. Capozello, and W. Shang. Washington, DC: American Bar Association Juvenile Justice Center.

Bishop, D. 2000. Juvenile offenders in the adult criminal justice system. In *Crime and Justice: A Review of Research,* edited by M. Tonry. Chicago, IL: University of Chicago Press, pp. 81–167.

Bishop, D., and Frazier, C. 2000. Consequences of transfer. In *The Changing Borders of Juvenile Justice: Transfer of Adolescents to the Criminal Court,* edited by J. Fagan and F. Zimring. Chicago, IL: University of Chicago Press.

Bishop, D., Frazier, C., Lanza-Kaduce, L., and Winner, L. 1996. The transfer of juveniles to criminal court: Does it make a difference? *Crime & Delinquency* 42:171–191.

Butterfield, F. 1995. *All God's Children.* New York, NY: Knopf.

Butts, J., and Travis, J. 2002. *The Rise and Fall of American Youth Violence: 1980 to 2000.* Washington, DC: Urban Institute.

Chung, H., Little, M., and Steinberg, L. 2005. The transition to adulthood for adolescents in the juvenile justice system: A developmental perspective. In *On Your Own Without a Net: The Transition to Adulthood for Vulnerable Populations,* edited by D.W. Osgood, E.M. Foster, C. Flanagan, and R. Gretchen. Chicago, IL: University of Chicago Press.

Clemmer, D. 1958. *The Prison Community.* New York, NY: Holt, Rinehart & Winston.

Collins, W.A., and Steinberg, L. 2006. Adolescent development in interpersonal context. In *Handbook of Child Psychology: Socioemotional Processes,* edited by W. Damon and N. Eisenberg. New York, NY: Wiley.

Cooke, D.J., and Michie, C. 2001. Refining the construct of psychopath: Toward a hierarchical model. *Psychological Assessment* 13(2):171–188.

DiIulio, J. 1995. The coming of the super-predators. *Weekly Standard* (November 27):23.

Eggleston, A. 2007. *Perceptual Punishment: The Consequences of Adult Convictions for Youth*. Washington, DC: Campaign for Youth Justice.

Fagan, J. 1996. The comparative advantage of juvenile versus criminal court sanctions on recidivism among adolescent felony offenders. *Law & Policy* 18:77–112.

Fagan, J. 2008. Juvenile crime and criminal justice: Resolving border disputes. *Future of Children* 18(2):81–118.

Fagan, J., and Zimring, F.E. 2000. *The Changing Borders of Juvenile Justice: Transfer of Adolescents to the Criminal Court*. Chicago, IL: University of Chicago Press.

Feld, B. 1977. *Neutralizing Inmate Violence: Juvenile Offenders in Institutions*. Cambridge, MA: Ballinger Publishing Company.

Forth, A., Kosson, D., and Hare, R. 2003. *The Hare Psychopathy Checklist: Youth Version, Technical Manual*. North Tonawanda, NY: Multi-Health Systems, Inc.

Gillespie, W. 2003. *Prisonization: Individual and Institutional Factors Affecting Inmate Conduct*. New York, NY: LFB Scholarly Publishing LLC.

Gottfredson, S.D., and Gottfredson, D.M. 1986. Accuracy of prediction models. In *Criminal Careers and "Career Criminals,"* edited by A. Blumstein, J. Cohen, J. Roth, and C.A. Visher. Washington, DC: National Academy of Sciences Press, pp. 212–290.

Greenberger, E., Josselson, R., Knerr, C., and Knerr, B. 1974. The measurement and structure of psychosocial maturity. *Journal of Youth and Adolescence* 4:127–143.

Griffin, P. 2003. *Trying and Sentencing Juveniles as Adults: An Analysis of State Transfer and Blended Sentencing Laws*. Pittsburgh, PA: National Center for Juvenile Justice.

Griffin, P. 2006. *National Overviews: State Juvenile Justice Profiles*. Pittsburgh, PA: National Center for Juvenile Justice.

Hansen, B. 2001. Kids in prison. *The CQ Researcher* 27:345–376.

Hartney, C. 2006. *Youth Under Age 18 in the Adult Criminal Justice System*. San Francisco, CA: National Council on Crime and Delinquency.

Jensen, E., and Metsger, L. 1994. A test of the deterrent effect of legislative waiver on violent juvenile crime. *Crime & Delinquency* 40:96–104.

Jones, S., Cauffman, E., Miller, J., and Mulvey, E. 2006. Investigating different factor structures of the Psychopathy Checklist: Youth version: Confirmatory factor analytic findings. *Psychological Assessment* 18:33–48.

Kelly, J. 2010. Justice initiates new study of juveniles transferred to adult courts. *Youth Today* (November/December):31.

Kupchik, A., Fagan, J., and Liberman, A. 2003. Punishment, proportionality, and jurisdictional transfer of adolescent offenders: A test of the leniency gap hypotheses. *Stanford Law and Policy Review* 14:57–83.

Kurlychek, M.C., and Johnson, B.D. 2004. The juvenile penalty: A comparison of juvenile and young adult sentencing outcomes in criminal court. *Criminology* 42(2):485–517.

Kurlychek, M.C., and Johnson, B.D. 2010. Juvenility and punishment: Sentencing juveniles in adult criminal court. *Criminology* 48(3):725–757.

Lane, J., Lanza-Kaduce, L., Frazier, C.E., and Bishop, D.M. 2002. Adult versus juvenile sanctions: Voices of incarcerated youths. *Crime & Delinquency* 48:431–455.

Levitt, S.D. 1998. Juvenile crime and punishment. *Journal of Political Economy* 106(6):1156–1185.

Loughran, T., and Mulvey, E.P. 2010. Estimating treatment effects: Matching quantification to the question. In *Handbook of Quantitative Criminology,* edited by A. Piquero and D. Weisburd. New York, NY: Springer, pp. 163–181.

Loughran, T.A., Mulvey, E.P., Schubert, C.A., Chassin, L., Steinberg, L., Piquero, A.R., Cota-Robles, S., Fagan, J., Cauffman, E., and Losoya, S.H. 2010. Differential effects of adult court transfer on juvenile offender recidivism. *Law and Human Behavior* 34(6):476–488.

Loughran, T., Piquero, A.R., Fagan, J., and Mulvey, E.P. 2012. Differential deterrence: Studying heterogeneity and changes in perceptual deterrence among serious youthful offenders. *Crime & Delinquency* 58(1):3–27.

Males, M.A. 2008. Myths and facts about "direct file," minorities, and adult-court sentencing. Available online: www.cjcj.org/post/juvenile/justice/myths/and/facts/about/direct/file/minorities/and/adult/court/sentencing/0.

Maruna, S., and Toch, H. 2005. The impact of imprisonment on the desistance process. In *Prisoner Reentry and Crime in America,* edited by J. Travis and C. Visher. New York, NY: Cambridge University Press.

McGowan, A., Hahn, R., Liberman, A., Crosby, A., Fullilove, M., Johnson, R., Moscicki, E., Price, L., Snyder, S., Tuma, F., Lowy, J., Briss, P., Cory, S., and Stone, G. 2007. Effects on violence of laws and policies facilitating the transfer of juveniles from the juvenile justice system to the adult justice system: A systematic review. *American Journal of Preventative Medicine* 32(4s):S7–S28.

McShane, M.D., and Williams, F.P. 1989. The prison adjustment of juvenile offenders. *Crime & Delinquency* 35(2):254–269.

Monahan, K.C., Steinberg, L., Cauffman, E., and Mulvey, E.P. 2009. Trajectories of antisocial behavior and psychosocial maturity from adolescence to young adulthood. *Developmental Psychology* 45(6):1654–1668.

Mulvey, E. 2011. *Highlights From Pathways to Desistance: A Longitudinal Study of Serious Adolescent Offenders.* Washington, DC: U.S. Department of Justice, Office of Justice Programs, Office of Juvenile Justice and Delinquency Prevention.

Mulvey, E., and Schubert, C. 2012. Youth in prison and beyond. In *Oxford Handbook on Juvenile Crime and Juvenile Justice,* edited by B. Feld and D. Bishop. New York, NY: Oxford University Press, pp. 843–867.

Mulvey, E., Schubert, C., and Chung, H.L. 2007. Service use after court involvement in a sample of serious adolescent offenders. *Children and Youth Services Review* 29:518–544.

Myers, D. 2003. The recidivism of violent youths in juvenile and adult court: A consideration of selection bias. *Youth Violence and Juvenile Justice* 1(1):79–101.

National Prison Rape Elimination Commission Report. 2009. Available online: www.ncjrs.gov/pdffiles1/226680.pdf.

Oyserman, D., and Fryberg, S.A. 2006. The possible selves of diverse adolescents: Content and function across gender, race and national origin. In *Possible Selves: Theory, Research, and Application,* edited by C. Dunkela and J. Kerpelman. Huntington, NY: Nova Science Publishers.

Penney, S.R., and Moretti, M.M. 2005. The transfer of juveniles to adult court in Canada and the United States: Confused agendas and compromised assessment procedures. *International Journal of Forensic Mental Health* 4(1):19–37.

Petersilia, J., Turner, S., Kahan, J., and Peterson, J. 1985. Executive summary of RAND's study, "Granting felons probation: Public risks and alternatives." *Crime & Delinquency* 31:379–392.

Pogarsky, G., and Piquero, A.R. 2003. Can punishment encourage offending? Investigating the "resetting" effect. *Journal of Research in Crime and Delinquency* 40:95–120.

Redding, R.E. 1999. Examining legal issues: Juvenile offenders in criminal court and adult prison. *Corrections Today* (April):92–123.

Redding, R.E. 2008. *Juvenile Transfer Laws: An Effective Deterrent to Delinquency?* Washington, DC: U.S. Department of Justice, Office of Justice Programs, Office of Juvenile Justice and Delinquency Prevention.

Reynolds, C.R., and Richmond, B.O. 1985. *Revised Children's Manifest Anxiety Scale: RCMAS Manual.* Los Angeles, CA: Western Psychological Services.

Rosenbaum, P.R., and Rubin, D.B. 1983. The central role of the propensity score in observational studies for causal effects. *Biometricka* 70:41–55.

Schubert, C.A., Mulvey, E.P., Loughran, T., Fagan, J., Chassin, L., Piquero, A., Losoya, S., Steinberg, L., and Cauffman, E. 2010. Predicting outcomes for transferred youth: Implications for policy and practice. *Law and Human Behavior* 34(6):460–475.

Scott, E., and Steinberg, L. 2008. *Rethinking Juvenile Justice.* Cambridge, MA: Harvard University Press.

Sickmund, M. 1994. *How Juveniles Get to Criminal Court.* Washington, DC: U.S. Department of Justice, Office of Justice Programs, Office of Juvenile Justice and Delinquency Prevention.

Singer, S.I. 1996. *Recriminalizing Delinquency: Violent Juvenile Crime and Juvenile Justice Reform.* New York, NY: Cambridge University Press.

Singer, S.I., and McDowell, D. 1988. Criminalizing delinquency: The deterrent effects of the New York Juvenile Offender Law. *Law & Society Review* 22:521–535.

Spelman, W. 2000. What recent studies do (and don't) tell us about imprisonment and crime. In *Crime and Justice: A Review of Research,* edited by M. Tonry. Chicago, IL: University of Chicago Press, pp. 419–494.

Strom, K.J. 2000. *Profile of State Prisoners Under Age 18, 1985–97.* Washington, DC: U.S. Department of Justice, Office of Justice Programs, Bureau of Justice Statistics.

Tanenhaus, D.S. 2000. The evolution of transfer out of the juvenile court. In *The Changing Borders of Juvenile Justice,* edited by J. Fagan and F.E. Zimring. Chicago, IL: University of Chicago Press, pp. 13–44.

Tanenhaus, D.S. 2004. *Juvenile Justice in the Making.* New York, NY: Oxford University Press.

Walden, T.A., Harris, V.S., and Catron, T.F. 2003. How I feel: A self-report measure of emotional arousal and regulation for children. *Psychological Assessment* 15(3):399–412.

Weinberger, D.A., and Schwartz, G.E. 1990. Distress and restraint as superordinate dimensions of self-reported adjustment: A typological perspective. *Journal of Personality* 58(2):381–417.

Winner, L., Lanza-Kaduce, L., Bishop, D., and Frazier, C. 1997. The transfer of juveniles to criminal court: Re-examining recidivism over the long term. *Crime & Delinquency* 43(4):548–563.

Woolard, J.L., Odgers, C., Lanza-Kaduce, L., and Daglis, H. 2005. Juveniles within adult correctional settings: Legal pathways and developmental considerations. *International Journal of Forensic Mental Health* 4:1–18.

Young, M.C., and Gainsborough, J. 2000. *Prosecuting Juveniles in Adult Court: An Assessment of Trends and Consequences.* Washington, DC: The Sentencing Project.

Zimring, F.E. 1998. *American Youth Violence.* New York, NY: Oxford University Press.

Zimring, F.E. 2005. *American Juvenile Justice.* New York, NY: Oxford University Press.

Acknowledgments

Edward P. Mulvey, Ph.D., is Professor of Psychiatry and Director of the Law and Psychiatry Program at the Western Psychiatric Institute and Clinic (WPIC), University of Pittsburgh School of Medicine. Carol A. Schubert, M.P.H., is the Research Program Administrator of the Law and Psychiatry Program at WPIC.

Share With Your Colleagues

Please direct comments and/or questions to:
National Criminal Justice Reference Service
P.O. Box 6000
Rockville, MD 20849–6000

800–851–3420
301–519–5600 (fax)
Web:
tellncjrs.ncjrs.gov

This bulletin was prepared under grant number 2007–MU–FX–0002 from the Office of Juvenile Justice and Delinquency Prevention (OJJDP), U.S. Department of Justice.

Points of view or opinions expressed in this document are those of the authors and do not necessarily represent the official position or policies OJJDP or the U.S. Department of Justice.

The Office of Juvenile Justice and Delinquency Prevention is a component of the Office of Justice Programs, which also includes the Bureau of Justice Assistance; the Bureau of Justice Statistics; the National Institute of Justice; the Office for Victims of Crime; and the Office of Sex Offender Sentencing, Monitoring, Apprehending, Registering, and Tracking.